Sweet Remorse

Laura Avadyaev

BookLeaf Publishing

India | USA | UK

Presentation by *BookLeaf Publishing*

Web: www.bookleafpub.com

E-mail: info@bookleafpub.com

ISBN: 9789363317062

First edition 2024

To myself for trying, from his blessings.

The Rain

The rain brings the sound of
drops hitting the ground.

Hitting a surface
Music to the ears
Music to the soul
Touching the skin
Watering life, our life

The silence is what allows the
rain drops to be heard.
Our sense of hearing
Do you hear it?

Soothing to the mind
When the thoughts are finally
silent but the rain.
Peace has arrived

Summer June

Not too hot but has just about the right breeze
going along the waves.
Not too colorless but has plenty of vibrant
flowers and greens.
Not too loverless but brings lovers together.

Days filled with sunlight, warmth, and beautiful
butterflies.
Light intake, nostalgic feelings, increasing our
serotonin.
Making these stretched days more blissful and
saved within.

Summer has the breathtaking sunrise to the wake
of birds singing our song.
A sweet melody to the ears while lovers shine
through the eyes.
Summer has the radiant sunset with nights, we
hope to share it with the one.
Where lovers come together.

The one we can continue our dream with.
Lifelong, forevermore.
All is left is for the one, that's missing this
Summer June.

Soul Wanderers

We are here
We are there
We want to be there
But where is that.
Where is there?

Feels like we are being pulled in all directions.
The tired of feeling bones loosen as the force
takes its call.

Not every wanderer is lost.
Perhaps the soul feeds its crave through the
unknown.
Feels energized, a genuine high.
But for how long?
Until it diminishes
But what then?

Keep floating until the force reappears.
Maybe this time the soul wanderers will have a
place.
A place, not where is there but what is there.

Nefes

While we are here
We keep moving forward.
We try to keep up.
We try to embrace our downfall
To get back up again.
The intentions are clear
But is it…
Without our breath
We are nothing.
Nothing but lifeless.
So keep moving forward
As long it's still there.

Gone & Away

The dead isn't near, they are far.
We burden ourselves with the effort of the
unwanted and leave the dead tucked away.
We have time for the unfortunate tasks but don't
have the time for the pleasing ones.
We say there is always tomorrow.
Is there?

The dead is screaming to wake up. Wake up and
do the unforgettable.
Hear their screams and cries, after all they are
the angels circling us.
The dead may be far but are they, in fact they are
near.
Watching and listening, untimed and endlessly.
Remember that!

Don't leave the dead behind you, leave their
spirits alive.
Feel them!

Sweet Remorse

Life has been good
Life has been difficult
Life has been true
Life has been deceitful
Life has been visionary
Life has been bitter
Life has given her all
But has taken as well
Life has been sorry
Life has been angry
Life has been well
Life has been awry
Life has been warm
Life has been cold
Life has been kind
Life has been teary,
Both the happy and sad kind
Life has been a living fire
But life will always be here
And always hoping for the best.
Life is a sweet remorse.

The Light

To myself, who constantly challenges within
oneself.
Remember every day is another breath, given.

Where does it shine.
Where does it hide.
Point towards the direction.

Is it only a one way direction.
Or can we turn back.
Speak!

Will there be a detour.
Or only dark circles.

Is going through the tunnel necessary.
Is distance meant to be kept.
Will cutting through the woods, help.
To avoid some signs.
Avoid some signs.
Speak!

Are there any sparks that can be channeled.
There will be light. Even for a short period.
Don't put out the fire just yet.

That Time

Remember that time we had smiles sliding down
the slide or swinging high to reach the sky.

Remember that time we had butterflies going
down a hill on those deserted roads.

Remember that time we had giggles when a
friend would trip or after slipping some salt into
their drinks.

Remember that time we tried a new flavor of
sweet and craved more until it became our spot.

Remember that time we almost peed in our pants
laughing so hard to white chicks.

Remember that time we cruised to the mountains
for that sunrise and felt high from no sleep.

Remember that time we fell in love, thinking it's
forever.

Remember that time we found ourselves with a
broken heart from that forever.

Remember that time when we lost a loved one to the earth and had to keep going.

Remember that time we became who we are all within time.

Remember that time…

Lost In Thoughts

When does it stop
That feeling
That feeling of failure
That feeling of void
That feeling of the unknown
When does it stop?

People thinking they understand what others go
through or what they have been through.
Other then that we find ourselves in some of
them.
But can we measure pain
No
Can we measure the mind
No
Can we measure feelings
No

We just share what we are made of, flesh and
bones and life that was given to us.
Can the mind control feelings,
That would be controversial.

It's the what if, the guilt, the wondering, the
regrets, the risk taken or not, the constant
thinking that's never ending.
Like a broken record on repeat.

It keeps some of us in a loop of awareness but
battles every thought.
Challenges that need to be overcome.
Peace thrown out the window every time.

We cling to a source to help try to get us out of
that funk, even just for a little.
A temporary fix, a safe haven.
But that right there is gold.
Find that source that won't keep you lost in
thoughts even further but keeps you at ease.

Days

Days filled with smiles
Days filled with sadness
Days filled with giggles
Days filled with cries
Days filled with punctuality
Days filled with delays
Days filled with risks
Days filled with regrets
Days filled with love
Days filled with hate
Days filled with strength
Days filled with weakness
Days filled with courage
Days filled with cowardliness
Days filled with happiness
Days filled with anger
Days filled with lives
Days filled with chances
Days are how we make it.
Choose your day and fill it…

Green Eyes

His eyes smile
His eyes lie
His eyes love
But tells another story
His eyes shine
But hidden with a message
His green eyes will keep you wondering
But the light in his eyes will always remain

Traveler

Time doesn't stop but races
We have this one lifetime to fulfill
With the hope of making it, a success

We travel through time, through life as if we
have more seconds in the minute, more minutes
in the hour.

But for some it's given the opportunity to correct
and for some like a thrown rock in the ocean
hoping it will remain lost and never discovered.

We choose who to be. We travel through days,
months, years to decide which role to play,
which part to act, and which ending to finish
with.

It can be fun, it can be silly, it can be scary,
It can be boring, it can be loving, it can be
passionate,
It can be memorable, it can be precious, it can be
sad.
But for some it can just be temporary stages
until we find the right fit all in time.

So travel back in time and travel through time
with how things can be
Flashbacks that races through the eyes can help
achieve what should be, what shouldn't be, and
what should be forgotten.

Time reveals

The Sound

Ducks quacking, trying to win an argument.
Planes racing through the sky, scaring the clouds
with its speed.
The sun reflecting of one end of the world
through the channels of the waves.

Remember that day, days…

The breeze that blows the birds into a race.
The tide overflowing what's left of the sand.
The drifters that growl a cry for help, all in 360,
leaving its mark for days.

The sound of the ocean
The bubbles that form
The shells, the rocks, the dirt it brings to the
surface
Only to wash away once more
The waves flowing in its highs and lows
Only growing more forceful

The sound, only grows stronger
But never does it conquers the silence,
The silence of the mind but the sea.

Lone Lion

Some days he appears to have love, warmth,
laughters, good times, shine in his eyes, he cares
Some days he appears to have guilt, remorse,
arguments, lies, tears

Why is that
Is there an internal void
Is there an internal scarring
What shifts one to lead towards
being someone hurtful.
Is he a scared individual,
A intimated individual,
An ego feeder,
An anxiety feeler,
A wounded soul
Easily persuaded

Who is he
Not a healer
But looks for his temporary fix
Often
Although he could have healed
But was closed to it
He was a runaway
When overwhelmed

The inability to stand and fight for what's right,
for love, for life, for a strong future, for the
extraordinary

Sadly, as long as he remains to give in to a
cowardly side
He will remain as the lone Lion I will never
forget

Words As Weapons

The tongue
A organ that speaks
Speaks powerful words
Speaks empty words
Speaks passionate words
Speaks hatred words
Speaks memorable words
Speaks terrifying words
Speaks plenty
The good and the bad

Once it's out, it can't be tamed
Can't be taken back
No magical reset button to what is said,
Ever

Depending on what the tongue speaks
It's one of two things
Happy words or sad words
If it's something that can hurt
Surely think before speaking
Words can carry on within the mind and soul
Once heard never forgotten in the subconscious

The tongue is powerful
Holds the key to many doors
Refrain from using words as weapons
It's damaging to the soul species of humane
If trigger is pulled

The Unfortunates

In this world
There are both the sane and insane
In this world
There are both the healthy and unhealthy
In this world
We live a challenge life
We live to survive
We live to feel
We live to love
We live to be happy

But what of the unfortunates one
The ones that were semi blessed and have
disabilities
What of them
How do they perceive the world, the life,
Us
Do they understand
Within their minds, their hearts, their souls
Did their soul choose this path to look away
from all the wrong
In this world, this life,
Us

If that, are they truly blessed
For the soul is whole
And yearns for nothing more to just be
As the almighty's child, gracefully

We "the fortunates" are the semi blessed

Alone

The lonely duck
Wanders alone
In a lonely lake
Not known to many
Besides any passersby if any
With the lonely trees that are left
With the broken branches

Is he content
Is he afraid
Where are his friends
Where is his family
Will they come back for him

Does he dream of the what ifs
Does he dream of love
Or only the unknown
And the impossible
Why doesn't he fly to the unknown
Make a life, find the answers
Because the lake and the trees that are left, will
stay alone

The Hug

Seconds long
Memorable scent
Warm
Tight
Heart pounding
Rapid pulse
Safe
Home

Together

25

The dark, always thinks

The light, always wise

But it's never a pick and choose option at first

It comes together

It's easier to see the light when darkness has fell
upon us

Then we choose

The Flame

Flickers all directions,
Like a compass

Looking for a way out
Which way to go

Am I lost

Or looking for a way out

Wild Wind

Always around, always there
Feel surrounded, all directions

Warm or cold
Which one is it, this time

Day or night
Which one is it, this time

Where do I feel it
Where is it felt

Everywhere,
Where it has been touched